If you have purchased this book without its cover, it may be a stolen book. This should be reported to the publisher.

This publication is written and is intended to provide reliable and competent information. Neither the publisher or the author is under any obligation to provide professional services in rendering financial, legal or any related book content advice or otherwise.

The law and practices vary from country to country and state to state.

If legal or professional information is required, the purchaser or the reader should seek the information privately and best suited to their particular needs and circumstances.

The author and the publisher specifically disclaim any liability that may be incurred from the information and names used within this book.

The book contains a collection of case studies viewed from the researcher's perspective only. However, certain areas may have been enhanced for content purposes.

All rights reserved.

No part of this book, including the interior design, cover design, diagrams, or any intellectual property (IP) and icons may be reproduced or transmitted in any form by any means (electronic, photocopying, recording or otherwise) without the prior permission of the publisher.

ISBN: 978-0-6480836-2-7
Copyright© 2015 re-print 2017 Christine Thompson-Wells
All rights reserved.

Published by Books For Reading On Line.Com, under license from MSI Ltd, Australia

Company Registration No: 642923859
Australia
See our website: www.booksforreadingonline.com
Or contact by email: admin@booksforreadingonline.com

Front & Back Covers and Copyright owned by MSI, Australia

Content	Page
Chapter One How Selling Starts	1
Chapter Two A Different Idea And Business Approach	15
Chapter Three Establishing Your Business In The Market Place	32
Chapter Four Working With The Tools You Need In The Marketplace In Order To Sell	51
Chapter Five Radio, Television Advertising And The Worldwide Web (www)	75
Chapter Six Communication And Information In The 21st Century	88
Chapter Seven Selling Is An Ancient Custom	106
Bibliography	116

Chapter One

How Selling Starts

Like most things, selling starts with a thought. The thought develops into ideas of making, producing or developing a thing that, you in turn, can sell in the exchange for money.

The ideas of buying and selling are not new and have been around for thousands of years and well before biblical times, in fact, it's possibly about fifty-thousand years ago when the first markets are thought to have started up. It's from that time, human beings realized they had human needs which had to be satisfied to ensure their survival or add some creature comforts to their lives.

These people also realized if they could not provide the needs for themselves, they would need to buy, barter or steal them from other people!

Human needs are no different today than at the time of fifty-thousand years or so ago!

- ❖ *We all **need** to eat, drink, rest and play at different times in our daily lives.*

I would assume by buying and reading this book, you have identified a human **need** and you want to take your product, produce or services into the market place to see if you can sell it or advance in your selling career!

People will be interested in what you have to sell if

- ✓ its pleasing to the eye
- ✓ it has appeal and
- ✓ is affordable to them at the time

In Developing A Business - Market Test Your Produce, Product or Service

All produce or products need to be market tested. Market testing means making the minimum number of items you intend to sell. From developing a phone system, to developing face creams and body lotions or your latest designs in the clothing industry!

Remember, even with Market Testing, there is no guarantee that the item will be a success.

However, testing minimum numbers means you can run trials or carry out a range of different samples of your ideas without it costing you too much money.

As with all selling, whether you are starting a small business, or selling and working in a paid job, you need to be: sharp and sensitive to your client or customer's needs and wants. To sell you need to know your products, produce or services *'inside out'*.

Let's take these ideas a little deeper and I'll introduce you to Mary and Joe.

Joe had the idea of opening a café in a seaside resort. Joe was interested in making gluten-free biscuits and cakes but also other, but different, foods. It was a great idea, but the world's economy had just been hit by the 2008 world recession. Joe thought, waited and pondered for a while about his first ideas!

When you are thinking of selling anything, you need to look at what is happening around you and what's happening in the market place? You need to ask the questions: 'will my product, produce or services sell under these conditions?'

Mary on the other hand, had listened to Joe's idea but liked her idea of making chocolates better. Mary's idea, she thought, '*...feels comfortable for me'*. Mary's ideas were to make exclusive chocolates.

Both Mary and Joe decided to test their ideas out.

Joe was going to test his idea at the local markets, which run on a Sunday, and Mary was going to test her ideas out by going into the city and going to exclusive shops, including department stores.

Both were busy in the kitchen, Joe was making his gluten-free cakes and biscuits and Mary started to make her chocolates.

Mary's chocolates, when she had finished, were immaculate with tiny iced flowers and chocolate sculptures decorating them. Her chocolates were in milk and plain chocolate and some had a fresh cream, liquor or fruit fillings.

Joes, biscuits and cakes, when cooked, were also looking good – he counted six biscuits and put each lot of six into clear cellophane bags which were tied with clean, new natural string. He also put one cake in a separate cellophane bag and again tied them in the same way as the biscuits.

It was early Sunday morning and Joe loaded up his car with his trays of biscuits and cakes, trestle tables, table cloths of checkered material a chair and what he thought he needed to last the five hours of market trading. He drove the fifty minute drive and on reaching the market, set up his tables ready for selling his products.

Joe was excited, he had wanted to run his own business for a while and now he felt he had taken the first step!

Mary, meanwhile had decided to have a semi-lazy day and thought, 'I'll get ready for my trip into the city, tomorrow, Monday'.

During last week, she had telephoned a number of large, but fairly exclusive shops, spoken to the

Managers, and had appointments to meet the Managers all tomorrow, Monday.

She had very nice gift boxes made with her own signature: '*Heavenly Chocolates*' on the lid and each box contained six chocolates: one of each of her selection.

Meanwhile, Joe had his first customers at the market, he was happy. People wanted to speak with him and they wanted to know about his product. They asked questions like:

- ➢ What sort of flour do you use?
- ➢ Are your ingredients grown locally?
- ➢ Do you make them all yourself?
- ➢ How long will they last if I buy them today?
- ➢ Do your biscuits contain butter?
- ➢ Do you use milk in your cakes?

And so the questions continued to be asked by the market customers.

Some of the people looking at Joe's products said, 'that's a great idea, will you be back next week?'

Some people just looked at Joe's stand and decided to walk on to the next stall.

It was getting close to the time to pack up and Joe started to look at his money takings. He was a bit disappointed when he saw how much money was in the box. He thought to himself, 'I've hardly covered the cost of my ingredients!'

Disappointed, he packed up his stand and got ready for the drive home.

By the time he got home, Mary was in high spirits. She had her boxes of chocolates packed and ready for her trip into the city in the morning.

Joe briefly spoke to her about his experience at the market she listened politely, but couldn't help feeling her own excitement about her journey into the city the next day!

Mary had been in retail before and understood a lot about people and communication. Mary was aware that she needed to be:

- ✓ Able to talk about the ingredients in her product!
- ✓ Able to tell the Managers where her ingredients were grown and the conditions they were grown under!
- ✓ How many chocolates she could supply for busy times like Christmas, Easter and the holiday periods!
- ✓ How long the chocolates would last without refrigeration or if they needed refrigeration!
- ✓ What types of fillings she could make and what the range would be!

Mary had made a list of different fillings and types of chocolates: plain and milk, gluten-free, or sugar-free, and all of this was in a software package called 'Publisher'.

She had designed the list with copies of her photographed chocolates and printed it out on very nice card to give to the Managers.

Her head was in a spin as Joe tried to explain how his day had been.

Mary spoke to Joe and encouraged him to give his market stand another go the following Sunday. Joe thought about her suggestion and decided to try again the following week.

It was Monday morning and Mary was heading off early; she wanted to avoid the crowds and get into the city on time; she managed to do all of this.

She got to her first appointment and met Mr Fuller. Mr. Fuller was a fairly stout man but knew his business when it came to chocolates and confectionary. Mary produced her well displayed boxes of chocolates and Mr. Fuller immediately showed interest in what he was seeing.

His comment was, '....they look very nice but how do they taste Mary?' Mary replied, 'I think they taste nice, but I will have to wait and let you judge their taste!' She waited while Mr. Fuller ate the first chocolate.

Mary could feel her heart beating in her chest and she felt a fluster and then she felt anxious and thought, 'What if he doesn't like my chocolates?'

Mr. Fuller tried the first chocolate, and then had a sip of water, he tried the second, again, he had a sip of water, then the third and fourth and so on.

Mary sat waiting for his comments. He then replied, 'I think these are excellent Mary, but will they always taste as good as these?'

Many people trial their products and then put it out to a sub-contractor to make and produce in larger quantities. Small changes in the recipe or produce used to create the product can make a difference and interfere with the original taste.

The sub-contractor may not make the product exactly as it was originally intended to be made; even the way the blending of the recipe can make a difference in taste – if variations in flavor take place, it can kill a product in its tracks.

Overview

Joe did a lot of thinking during the Monday while Mary was in the city showing her chocolates to the Managers of the city stores.

The Story
For the following Sunday, Joe had different ideas. He wanted to do better than he had done the previous week. He decided to give some samples of his biscuits and cakes away to the market visitors.

He would be handing out nicely displayed biscuits and cakes and was continually thinking of how he could make positive changes to add more to his products. He wanted to make more sales than the previous week!

There are several things Joe can do at this point, he can:

- ✓ Broaden his range of products to include, but not be exclusive to gluten-free products – not all people are gluten intolerant.
- ✓ He could add to sell many varieties of preserves from picked local fruits.
- ✓ He may wish to run cooking classes or add to repertoire by giving away recipes – not the recipes of the product he sells but something which could be of use to the customer.
- ✓ He could also go into packaging raw ingredients for particular recipes which allow the customer to 'Just Add Water' and cook.

By Joe doing this, he has a greater market appeal. He can vary his range of products and make different cakes and biscuits weekly. He could also have 'Weekend Specials' or use, 'In Season,' fresh fruits in his recipes. Other broader avenues could include using: grated chocolate toppings or simply become more creative with the product.

While Mary was away, Joe continued to think about how he could make his ideas work.

Overview

Mary had arrived home on the Monday and was excited about her visits to the city stores.

Mary had made five visits to Managers and had secured four sales of twelve boxes of mixed chocolates to be delivered to each store the following week.

Mary worked on her orders getting, all the ingredients together ready to make her chocolates the following Saturday and Sunday. Sunday came and Mary was busy getting her chocolates ready for delivery on the Monday while Joe was at the market selling his products.

The Story

Mary put the finishing touches to her chocolates on Sunday afternoon; she looked down at her work and felt a great sense of pride in what she had created.

Joe had arrived home after his time at the market and was doing some serious thinking about his new business ideas.

Mary delivered her orders on the Monday as she had promised, left the invoices with each order for the Managers and waited to hear the outcome for the sales.

She waited for two weeks before she heard from the Mr. Fuller; she was surprised when she heard his voice. He said, 'it's nice to hear you Mary' and without a break in his speech, he continued, '...now your chocolates have been very popular and as its Easter in three weeks time, I would like to order fifty boxes of your mixed selections – is that OK?'

Mary could hardly believe her ears. It wasn't long after that, the phone rang again, and another Manager ordered thirty boxes. A week later, another Manager ordered a further twenty-five boxes.

Mary was now a very busy business woman.

Joe on the other-hand didn't like where he was going with his market produce and decided to help Mary with her business and to help her get through the busy period she was now facing.

Mary can now go in either one or two ways:

- ➢ She can continue to serve the existing customers in the four city shops she has or she can make it into a
- ➢ Commercial venture.

If Mary chooses to go commercially she would need to look at doing things differently.

- o She would need to do a **Business Task Plan.** She would need to outline a Business Plan - it's a bit premature for Mary to do an in-depth Business Plan on the current figures she has;

- o She would also need to think about where she's going and possibly think about creating a commercial kitchen to rent or buy and do her figures accordingly – This could be added into a non-complete Business Plan

Once a business becomes a commercial venture, at this point, a lot of money needs to be invested into the business to allow it to grow.

Mary was going to look at both possibilities after she had completed and delivered her Easter Orders.

Though Joe had tested his products in the market place, he wasn't covering his costs in

- ➢ Ingredients
- ➢ Fuel
- ➢ Stall hire at the market – he now needs to think his strategies through!

Outlined in this chapter are two case studies. The studies are of Mary and Joe – each had different ideas about the business venture they wanted to try out. As you progressed through the chapter, you will see the different outcomes which take place with different ideas and the different products produced.

What are your business plans?

YOUR NOTES

Chapter Two

A Different Idea And Business Approach

Setting up different businesses requires different approaches, strategies and different money spent.

Overview

Nigel has been interested in growing tomatoes ever since he was a boy. He said in a television interview, 'I just find tomatoes interesting and they are nice to eat and I'm fascinated by them!'

Nigel lives in the United Kingdom where his father grew vegetables for the local community.

The Story

Nigel's father had a small market garden where most vegetables were grown under glass. Out of all the produce his father grew, Nigel, liked the red tomato. The market garden gave the family a small income but they were not large vegetable producers.

As Nigel grew into adulthood, he took more interest in the humble red tomato. He had ideas, grand ideas, to make something small into something very large.

He did his research and knew to make his tomatoes grow larger and better, he needed to implement changes in his father's original ideas and his way of growing and working with vegetables.

Within the same area, about one and half kilometers away from market gardens, there is an industrial estate. Within the industrial estate is a sugar beet processing factory. This factory lets off a by-product from its production, the by-product being, CO_2 (carbon dioxide) in the form of hot water. Nigel was a bit of a brain when it came to chemistry, he knew he could get brighter, larger, healthier tomatoes if he could feed them with CO_2.

Arrangements were put into place between the sugar beet processing factory, the local council and Nigel to run a large pipeline of the by-product CO_2 from the processing factory to Nigel's glass houses.

The by-product of hot water containing CO_2 is transported around the glasshouses through purposely built installed piping. The hot water circulates around three hundred and sixty kilometers of glasshouses. The warmth within the glasshouses, in turn, gives a home to eight thousand bumble bees who fertilize the flowers of the tomato plants.

Nigel's dream came from a humble beginning and a vision he held within his mind. He put many ideas together and came up with a brilliant solution – he is now the largest tomato growing producer in the United Kingdom.

Many people have many ideas about what they want to achieve in life, not all plans work, but most do with modification and adaption and the vision to 'see the bigger picture'.

Nigel saw the 'bigger picture' with his tomato plants and knew more could be achieved through taking his initial thoughts further. Nigel needed to look at the thoughts he had, crystallize them into ideas and then work with the ideas to make them a reality.

Nigel needed to look at many areas of his business before going ahead with such a dream – the dream of heating and feeding his tomato plants. The ideas of *nicer looking, healthier, redder tomatoes* which were also *nicer tasting* were all thoughts that would have gone through his mind.

Let's take a look at how his ideas could have helped his business to become what it is today.

Nigel's Three Elements Of Success

- ✓ *Appearance:* Nigel would have thought about the look of his tomatoes. This is the start of the appearance factor in selling and relates to '*Presentation*' of the product. Because Nigel's plants look healthy and are healthy, people enjoy buying them and look forward to eating them. If the food looks good, feels good to touch: is firm and strong and the brightness of the colour of the tomato is

enticing, Nigel has hit the key factors in selling.
- ✓ *Healthy Eating:* is the image the food signifies and is paramount in selling food these days. People are more discerning now than ever before about the quality of their food. People want to know how their food is prepared and under what conditions it's grown. Nigel is using a healthy by-product of hot water to keep his greenhouses warm – his plants enjoy the conditions under which they grow, so they produce more and healthier fruit.
- ✓ *Taste:* taste is the last thing that the customer or client thinks about; a customer assumes: *'if it looks good, it must taste good'.* As you know, looks can be deceiving! For any food product to be successful, it must not only look good but taste better than it looks.

Before Nigel got to where he is today, he would have asked the following questions:

- ❖ is it viable?
- ❖ will it work?
- ❖ how will it work?

It's seen in the three previously mentioned case studies how different ideas are tried out, some work, some do not.

The three people: Joe, Mary and Nigel would have gone through the same questions when thinking about their business ideas and plans.

Nigel's tomato business may still be in the pre-days of a small market garden if he had not had 'Big Thoughts' and 'Big Ideas'.

Mary also has 'Big Ideas,' she has approached key department stores and exclusive shops to sell her chocolates. Joe has taken another approach but it could become very successful if he uses other strategies.

In all three cases, each person would be thinking about: *'How Much Is This Going To Cost?'*

Most businesses need an injection of money to kick start them; this is a difficult area for all new ideas.

Joe hasn't spent much money to find out there could be financial problems if he is to take his gluten-free cakes and biscuits further. It could become 'financially risky' if he is to pursue his ideas about opening a café at a seaside resort.

However, it doesn't mean that Joe should forget about his ideas at this point.

Mary has some serious thinking to do if she is to go ahead with her chocolate manufacturing ideas.

Nigel, however, has been a bit more fortunate in that his father has paved the way for him to take his ideas to a higher level.

Cost And On-Going Costs

To start in commercial business costs money. Some people start a business working with their credit cards and instantly create debt. This is risky and the business idea needs to instantly kick start.

With the start up of any business there is always

- ❖ Fit out costs

With the case of Mary, if she wants to take her business to the next level, she would need to:

a. Register her business name
b. Register for an ABN number or equivalent
c. Find a premises, which is council approved for food production
d. Install a commercial kitchen or equivalent
e. Formulate her Project Plan with the idea of creating a Business Plan from the information held within the Project Plan

In the case of Nigel, he would need to:

a. Have his business name and necessary paper work in place, this would include the company registration
b. He would work with the existing system his father created

    c. Adapt the ideas (possibly by increments – doing one thing at a time) so he doesn't interrupt the existing production or sales of the tomato crops.
    d. Formulate his ideas into a business Project Plan and then create a Business Plan

The Project Task Plan

By creating a Project Task Plan you can get a Big Picture of a small project. This is a simple process that works with any start-up business.

Simply:

1. Once you have thought about your thoughts which then become your business idea, write it down on a paper chart or create it on the Excel package on your computer.
2. Run your trials, date the information.
3. Cost out the money you have spent in the preparation of your product, include fuel, premises rental or stall hire.
4. Add up the income you have got for your efforts.
5. Take your expenses from your income and look at the difference – it will be either a minus or plus in your Profit or Loss.
6. You can make two columns for this or keep the information in the same column but record it in different colour ink.
7. Record customer reaction.

8. To be fair to yourself, you need to run trials over an eight week period or longer, never shorter.
9. Monitor yourself and don't forget to include the weather during the trial.

Mary's Idea – Project Task Plan

Idea: Making Hand-Made Chocolates – Record Any Modification/s To The Idea	Selling Date	Money Spent (Outgoings) On Ingredients & Costs	Income From Sales	Total Profit Or Loss Amount	Customer Reaction	The Weather	Your Comments

When you run your trials, use the above Project Plan to help keep you on track.

Business Plans

When you are asked by a bank or money lending authority to *'create a business plan,'* you are being asked to do a lot of work that rarely has any resemblance to what your outcome or expenses will be in the future.

Business Plans are acceptable to established businesses, but they are a 'tall order' for those businesses who are just starting out. Business Plans do have their value because they will extend your vision, however, *'the vision'* is not always the reality in the business world!

Nigel or his father would have gone through much of the above, but Joe and Mary are still in the early days of developing their businesses.

Trading Capital

More often than not, the most important part of any new business is the *Trading Capital* needed to keep a business going in the very early days.

Using Joe's business ideas: when Joe first went to the market to sell his biscuits and cakes he needed to cover his costs:

- Ingredients
- Fuel and
- Market stall cost. Looking a little closer:

➢ Cost of ingredients	$45.00
➢ Cost of fuel	$25.00
➢ Cost of market stall	$12.00

Joe needs to have in return for his effort:

$82.00

This is not profit, just income which will allow him to go back to the market next week should he think it's worthwhile for him to do so!

Taking the necessity of 'keeping in mind' *Trading Capital* expenses - every new business, when you leas or rent a commercial space, you need to break down your daily running expenses. You firstly need to identify the weekly expenses, for instance:

- Weekly rental of business premises $1,000.00
- If staff are employed $ 900.00
- Stock for the week $1,500.00
- Insurance & Public Risk $ 70.00
- Superannuation – staff $ 90.00

You will need to have income from your business

$3,560.00

These numbers are not paying you a wage or salary, so you will need to think carefully about your venture!

Now divide the amount by the number of days your business is operating; this will allow you to find the average daily income needed to keep you financially safe, remember, this is not your profit.

If you are working for six days a week, you will need an income of $593.00

a day.

Many businesses start up with no idea they will need Capital Trading Money for at least

- 3 Months
- 6 Months or
- 12 Months

Building into your Project Plan this element will help to keep you Financially Safe – however, there are no guarantees.

If your business is a new start up, you will need to look at

- ✓ Potential customers or clients
- ✓ Geographic location
- ✓ Geographic demographics – you will need to research:
    - o What is the disposable income of the area?
    - o Are people living in rental accommodation?
    - o Are people on the dole?
    - o Are they high income earners?
    - o Are there a number of private schools or state/public education schools in the community?
    - o What is the number of retiree's or divorced people in the community
    - o What is the average family number in the community?

- ✓ <u>Identify Your Region and Industry</u> - Are you working in 'Business to Business, in retail, research and development, Agriculture or Horticulture and associated industries, Health and Fitness or the services sector?'
- ✓ Product Affinity – Does your product, produce or services have a connection to peoples' good memories, (emotions)? If you have answered 'Yes,' to this point, you have *'Product Affinity?'*

Mary's 'Product Affinity' is All around the world 'People Love To Eat Chocolate'.

Nigel's 'Product Affinity' would be 'People Eat Tomatoes Because They Are Good For Them'. In some countries, because of the rich Vitamin C content of the fruit, people are known to call tomatoes: 'Heart Food'.

Joe is struggling with his product because he has a limited, but an enthusiastic customer base: the numbers of 'buying customers' are small and could be widely spaced within the community.

Joe's Inspiration

Joe could keep going with his idea, he could make contact with other food outlets; he may also approach independent supermarkets to see if they are interested in giving his product some 'shelf space'.

Gaining supermarket 'shelf space' is always a difficult process however it can and has been done with the 'right contact,' the 'right product' and to the 'right people' in place. Joe needs to take his time and approach the 'right' people. He needs to establish a profile for his product and become known for his 'whole food,' 'alternative food,' 'healthy food' approach and local weekend markets are a good way to start!

Joe hasn't been very impressed with the market approach to date, but he could try other markets and continue to test, test and test his product.

Mary's Dream

Mary is on her way to developing an 'exclusive,' 'market place' for her chocolates. If Mary is to grow her business, she may need to look at other city locations or outlets. Already mentioned, she would also need to establish herself in a small, commercial kitchen.

Things To Do When You Are Starting Your Business Or Going Into Selling!

Establishing Yourself In The Market Place

Make sure you have a clear idea of what you want to develop and sell – Mary has her chocolates, Joe his gluten-free cakes and biscuits and Nigel has his tomatoes.

- ✓ Test your product
- ✓ Test
- ✓ Test and
- ✓ Test

Once you are happy with your product, you can develop other 'add on' items.

Joe could develop other products: using locally grown fruit and vegetables and make jams, pickles and chutneys.

Mary, can expand her chocolates in many areas; she can add more flavours, exclude some flavors, add the 'love,' 'passion' image to her products and more.

Nigel's Choices

If Nigel wanted to diversify with his tomatoes, he could partner with a sauce company to take his 'out of shape' or rejected fruit to manufacture a number of different bottled tomato products such as healthy drinks, chutneys, pickles and relish.

Nigel, could also add the 'love,' 'passion' and 'health' image to his tomatoes.

Blindness By The Passion

When you are looking to go into business, you may become *'blinded by the passion'* to pursue your dreams.

The passion within human emotion which takes place during these times of excitement can distort the reality of the venture.

If you are experiencing high emotions and excitement with the ideas of your new venture, try to take a step backwards and review your situation. Look again, see where you are and ask yourself, 'are you prepared to meet all the costs and sacrifices the business or venture is going to throw at you?

You need your emotion to drive your venture, but many good ideas fall into heartbreaking shreds when the emotional drivers go out of control.

I have written at length about the Adult, Child and Parent Ego States in my books: *Adam's Mind – Eve's Psyche* and *Discover Your Selling Power*.

We've spent a lot of time speaking about the thought processes, dreams and reality of the situations for Joe, Mary and Nigel.

Without large capital investment, businesses need to grow organically. A Business like any other human venture needs to prove it's worthwhile for the person to continue with his or her dream.

Be cautious – are you listening to reality or your emotional drivers?

Think of your business and calculate the cost. A simple exercise is to make a batch of muffins and estimate the retail price you could charge for each muffin, take cost of ingredients, your time, and any other expenses you have incurred. Take the wholesale cost, from the retail income and you have your answer.

YOUR NOTES

Chapter Three

Establishing Your Business In The Marketplace – Selling

Once you are happy with your ideas and you have done your testing, you need to go to the next level.

This is the start of your *Branding Process.* Branding and becoming identifiable by your brand is an important step to establish your product in the *'market place'.* To become noticeable you need to be different but somehow, similar or 'somehow' the same as other products but you do need to establish your own *'Point Of Difference'.*

Mary has a *'Point Of Difference,'* though there are many chocolate manufacturers in the market place, Mary has developed her own uniquely and identifiable brand, or *'Point of Difference'.* Nigel has developed a *'Point Of Difference,'* with growing 'larger, redder and better tasting tomatoes;' Joe is however, still working with his ideas.

Becoming Noticed

Yellow Pages - Not all people agree these days on the validity of the Yellow Pages and Yellow Page advertising. It is however, a very worthwhile tool if you want to be at the 'finger tips' of your customers or clients.

Being in the Yellow Pages allows you, at a small and extra charge, to become linked to Google which will help your customers or clients find you via the internet.

However, being in the Yellow Pages may take time – Yellow Page Directories only come out once a year, so you would need to see when they close and when the next edition is out! If you go into business just as the new edition is coming out, you will probably have to wait a few months before your advertisement is seen by the general people in the community and on the internet and wait for the hard, paper format to be released later in the year.

Letters – Sending out letters is a cheap, but a viable way of letting people know you are now operating in business and have a new range of, for example: biscuits, cakes, chocolates, tomatoes, sauces, condiments or other products, services or produce for sale.

It normally takes three letters to make the contact with the customer or consumer. To be safe rather than sorry, find about thirty to fifty names and addresses and record them; write or type them into a data base. If you don't have any names or addresses, use the Yellow or White Pages of the Telephone Directories; this will help you identify future customers.

Record:

1. Title: Mr, Mrs, Sir, Madam, Colonel, Doctor, Professor etc
2. Initials
3. Name/s, including the person's initials
4. Addresses
5. Postcodes – postcodes may have to be looked up independently of the address – this can be done by entering: Postcode into Google.
6. Keep a spreadsheet or document, in a safe place; *remember, always be alert to data protection and privacy laws when collecting your information on other people.*
7. Continually add to your information.
8. Number each contact eg: 1 through to 50
9. When meeting contacts at business meetings - record all business contacts or acquaintances and their information – *(warning: not everybody will appreciate being contacted but some will appreciate your efforts and therefore give you the time you need to tell them about what you are doing.)* You may like to add some separate information which helps you to identify that person at a much later date. For example: Blond hair, Zoe - we had a coffee at the Coffee Club, Heavy moustache on Bill - sat next to him at the concert dinner and so on.

The Three Letter Introduction

3 Letters – Over a six to nine week period, make contact with your first customers or clients.

Send out:

1. Send out Letter Number One – *always record, and make notes of your actions.* Create a spread sheet or follow the example below.

Example Of Your Contact Or Data Collection For Your Business

Date	Title	Name	Address	Post Code	T: Number	M: Number	L 1	L 2	L 3	Your Comments
06 June-2012	Mr	Brown	25 Winchester Mews Surrey, UK	SU8 079	01189 624 5326	0457698 8836	✔			
"	Mrs	Green	16 Chester Avenue Surrey, UK	SU7 087	01189 768 4572					

The names, addresses and phone numbers above are fictitious but the idea will get you started.

Make a habit of recording your daily information – keep a diary handy this information can become a invaluable source as your business matures.

2. As in the above diagram, record the information from your letters on an Excel spreadsheet, make sure you keep a note of your comments;
3. Letter number two – send out three weeks later;
4. Letter number three – send out, allow the process of sending out letters to take about nine weeks.

The first letter should be light and an introduction to you and your venture – it is not a 'Sales Letter'. The KISS logic applies to sending out your three letters (Keep It Simple Stupid) - one page of information is sufficient and will be read, longer letters may end up in the bin!

In the first letter you need to outline what you and your business is about, how long you have lived in the area and any other information which will help you to establish your product and business.

Before sending out your letters give some samples of your products to your neighbours, and let them try it or them out. With the good information you receive back and with the permission from your neighbor/s, you can collect the data and use it as testimonials.

If your neighbours have given you their permission to use their name on the testimonial, use their name to validate your information. If they don't give you their permission to use their name, you can always use their good testimonial and genuinely say: '...my neighbours' are delighted with my chocolates and have already become customers. Never lie or exaggerate, but always be enthusiastic and honest with your written words.

By keeping the numbers of letters you work with small in the beginning, you can deliver and make personal contact with people.

Below are three numbered sample-letters, each is a process and allows you to work with your own information. Replace the necessary information with your own information – this letter needs to work with and for you.

Letter Number One - Sample

Your Name
Your Address

The Name and Address of Your New Customer

Date your letter, for example: 10th November 2012

Dear (Salutation) for example: Mrs Green

Introduce yourself:
My name is Mary Brown. I live in your neighbourhood and have recently started my own chocolate business.

I make hand-made chocolates with many different and exciting fillings. I use fresh, local fruit to make some of the chocolates and only use the best ingredients, in the marketplace, I can buy.

My neighbours have sampled my chocolates and they have made the following comments:

- ✓ 'Very nice, I will keep you in mind at Christmas time,' Alan White.
- ✓ 'Lovely, a true taste of chocolate, very nice indeed'. Dorothy Turnball

Because the chocolates are proving to be so popular, I have pleasure in leaving you these two samples, together with this letter of introduction. If you would like to contact me, my phone number is: 00 000 000.

Thank you for your time in reading this letter.
Sincerely

Mary Brown
Heavenly Chocolates

To really take advantage of the work you are doing, try where possible, to hand deliver your produce, products or the information on the services you are offering.

Letter Number Two - Sample

Your Name
Your Address

The Name and Address of Your New Customer

Date your letter, for example: 10th November 2012

Dear (Salutation) for example: Mrs Green

Three weeks ago, I made contact with you and left (gave) you two of my hand-made chocolates. I am pleased to say, my chocolates have been very well received by the neighbours in your street.

Because my business is now starting to expand, I am running 'Heavenly Chocolates' home tasting programs. I would like to offer you this introductory program. You can invite your close friends and relatives for this enjoyable event.

If this is not for you, would be kind enough to mention this offer to your family and friends.

At no cost or obligation to you, I would like to offer you two further free chocolates. As the Christmas season is nearly upon us, I would also like to offer you a discount of 20% off your Christmas order. Please see my Christmas Catalogue enclosed with this letter.

If you would like to contact me, my phone number is:
00 000 000.

Thank you for your time in reading this letter.
Sincerely

Mary Brown
Heavenly Chocolates

Letter Number Three – If There Is No Response to The First Two Letters - Sample

Your Name
Your Address

The Name and Address Of Your New Customer

Date your letter, for example: 2nd February 2013

Dear (Salutation) for example: Mrs Green

Invitation

Chocolate Tasting At Chocolatiere

'Chocolate Indulgence' The Village, Hampshire

I know how busy life can become, I therefore, would like you to accept these home made chocolates; these are from my new collection, and are for you to enjoy at your leisure.

At no obligation to yourself, I would also like to extend an invitation to our *'Chocolate Tasting'* morning at the local *Chocolatiere* 'Chocolate Indulgence' in the village at 10.00am on Saturday 9th March 2013.

'Chocolate Indulgence' is now selling my chocolates and this is a celebration to launch our new, exciting range.

It is important to know about numbers for this event, so if you can come along, please contact me - my phone number is: 00 000 000.

Thank you for your time in reading this letter.
Sincerely

Mary Brown
Heavenly Chocolates

Letter Number Three – When There Is A Response - Sample

Your Name
Your Address

The Name and Address Of Your New Customer

Date your letter, for example: 2nd February 2013

Dear (Salutation) for example: Mrs Green

Invitation

Chocolate Tasting At Chocolatiere,

'Chocolate Indulgence,' The Village, Hempshire

Because I value your custom, I would like to invite you to the above celebration.

At: 10.00am
On: Saturday 9th March 2013.

'Chocolate Indulgence' is now selling my chocolates and this is a celebration to launch our exciting, new range.

It is important to know about numbers for this event, so if you can come along, please contact me - my phone number is: 00 000 000.

Thank you for your time in reading this letter.
Sincerely

Mary Brown
Heavenly Chocolates

It's better to create a strong customer base rather than spreading yourself too thinly. Here Mary is concentrating on her local community.

She still has her City customers, but her local community could be her long-term customers or clients and these people are her direct cash flow base.

The letter is a valuable, cost effective tool and if you find it works for you and your product, produce or service, you can add more pages and really build up your story – people love a story!

Envelopes

We know from experience, if you send letters out, they <u>should not</u> look like a business letter with business promotional information, logos or any other related business emblems.

Promotional envelopes should be written by hand with <u>hand-written names and addresses.</u>

Follow-up research has shown, if junk mail (your advertising) looks like advertising, at least '*...50% of all clearly identifiable advertising solicitations and junk mail is thrown out in the mail room'*. Meaning, there is no attempt to deliver junk mail. (cited Dunn's quoted in the Wall Street Journal), Kennedy. (2008).

From Letters To Cards

A5 - 2 Sided Card – Is an easy way to let people know about your new venture. You can buy A4 and A5 card from any good stationery outlet – if you are using A4 card, use a guillotine to cut the card in half – do not cut the card with scissors as it can look unprofessional.

Design a small advertisement and use both the front and back of the card. You can use Microsoft Publisher to design your cards.

A5 Card Advertising – Sample – Card Front

Invitation
Heavenly Chocolates

We are now supplying our 'Heavenly Chocolates' to 'Chocolate Indulgence,' and would like to say 'thank you' for your support.

You are invited to join us in the celebration of our new collection of chocolates,

At Chocolatiere,
'Chocolate Indulgence,' The Village, Hempshire
At: 10.00am
On: Saturday 9th March 2013.

Because of numbers are limited, please contact 00 000 000, to confirm you will be joining us.

A5 Card Advertising – Sample – Card Back

Invitation
Heavenly Chocolates

We are delighted to invite you to sample our new range of chocolates At Chocolatiere, 'Chocolate Indulgence.

Our chocolates are made of the best and finest ingredients. We pride ourselves on creating sensational flavours that will arouse your senses!

Here are some of the exciting new flavours:

Wild Strawberry & Yogurt Cream, Mountain Lime & Ginger, Red Cherry & Brandy Cream, Orange & Coffee Essence.

Always Remember:

Message   Market   Media

Message

Your *message* must be clean, sharp and to the point. You must be honest in the words you write and speak.

The 'Message' stays with people, the words you speak become attached to the emotional experiences of your customers. Always remember, selling is an emotional reaction taken by your customers, your consumers or clients.

The Story

Many, if not all products, produce and services sell because a story is attached to the product being sold, so what is your story?

Mary has a story about the development of her chocolates.

Joe has a story about his product and his market visits and where he's going with his biscuits and cakes, and,

Nigel has his story about his large, red, healthy and good tasting tomatoes.

Market

By taking a look at Mary and her chocolate products, we know that chocolates are not for everybody. Mary would need to be sensitive to the 'needs' and 'wants' within her market place.

Many people don't eat chocolates because they believe by eating them they put on weight in a hurry! Mary could strengthen her message by supporting her product with market research.

> ➤ Eating a small amount of dark chocolate three times a week:
>   - ✓ Is good for your heart.
>   - ✓ Dark chocolate is good for your brain and improves your thinking powers.

- ✓ It allows your brain to release endorphins – endorphins allow you to feel good, healthy and alive.
- ✓ Dark chocolate also helps to control your blood-sugar level.
- ✓ Dark chocolate helps to harden tooth enamel.
- ✓ Dark chocolate also contains
  - ❖ Potassium
  - ❖ Copper
  - ❖ Magnesium
  - ❖ Iron, and

Dark chocolate helps in preventing Type 2 diabetes, high blood pressure and heart disease.

She may also say, 'her chocolate has:

- ✓ No Added sugar (Mary may add no added sugar to some of her range of chocolates).

The choice of the ingredients she uses in her products is hers, but her customers and clients will tell her what they want!

By understanding the ingredients or the materials that make up your product, and listening to what the market place is telling you, you are empowering the product to meet the 'needs and wants' of your customer, client or consumer.

When you are armed with such powerful information, you alone are endorsing your belief in what you are doing.

To allow yourself the time and confidence to start on your new venture, start with family and friends and then broaden your base to include home visits.

In Mary's letters above, we have given you suggestions of a 'way forward'.

By contacting your neighbours and offering a 'Get Together' For 'Chocolate Tasting,' Mary is offering a sensory experience. Sensory experiences are difficult to refuse, especially to the 'chocolate lover!'

Mary is also adding gifts for the hostess where she has offered a unique and well-presented box of chocolates for hosting the event.

Or, Joe could run a *'Taste The Difference'* event and incorporate 'Wine and Selected Cheese' tasting to go with his gluten-free products - adding yet again, something extra. Mary or Joe could donate some of the income, say 10% to a local charity! Most people, within the community, like to support 'a local charity'.

What Goes Around Comes Around – this is true of anything you do:

What Goes Around Comes Around. If you have only good intentions and are thinking of going into business or developing your selling career, always give a bit away, for instance: if Joe gives some biscuits or cakes to the people on the stand or stall next to him, he is endorsing his product. Also, Joe could give samples of his product to people passing by his market stall. Mary is doing just this in the promotion of her chocolates.

When you give something away, don't expect anything in return, let the product work for you. Follow-up contacts, but don't intimidate!

Media

Become a friend with the Media. If you decide to plan something, always invite the media: television, radio, newspapers. The media is always looking for good, local stories. Give or send to the media samples of your product, produce or information about what you are selling. By giving something away to the local media it allows you to become a friend, keep them on side, they are very valuable to you.

When you are selling for a living, you need to constantly gain the latest knowledge that is available in the market place and remember:

Message, Market And Media

The 'Message,' 'Market' and 'Media' have to fit together like pieces of a jigsaw puzzle and it's your responsibility to make them work in unison.

If you are selling for a living or thinking of going into business, you now need to gain more skills and have a better understanding of what you want to receive in return for your effort and investment in time and money!

You will also need to become media 'savvy!'

When you are effectively selling for a living, you are using many skills, a great amount of personal energy, and you're always looking for and gaining extra knowledge.

Selling for a living is a challenge, its fun and can be an exciting journey of personal discovery.

If you have chosen your product to sell, how can you prepare your media coverage?

YOUR NOTES

Chapter Four

Working With The Tools You Need In The Marketplace In Order To Sell

Most people in the world sell something for their living. The artist sitting quietly painting his or her latest picture is possibly hoping to sell their work at the next Art Sale or Art Show. An artist does not often accept the fact that they are indeed a merchant. They, the artist, like us all, want to be paid for the time, effort and talent they put into creating their product/s; they too, are hoping to sell their art in exchange for money.

The Queen of England is selling her time, her image as the Monarch in exchange for tourism income and England's place in the world – she has been a long-term, paid Public Servant for over sixty years.

From the Queen to the artist or the woman working on the local supermarket checkout as an employee, you and me, we are all giving our time in exchange for payment in money or 'kind' and the 'currency of exchange'.

Take a few minutes and think, what did you do and you didn't get paid with money but you did it (the job), because it needed to be done! There is always a 'currency of exchange' for the effort you put into doing something!

The 'currency of exchange' may be in:

- ✓ Making you feel better because you needed to do a job you've been putting off;
- ✓ The reward for washing the dirty football shirt and shorts may be a kiss on the cheek but it's still a payment and 'thank you' and a 'currency of exchange,'
- ✓ Just the word 'thank you,' is also a payment and recognition of your effort – a 'currency of exchange'.

Craft Your Message

When you *'Craft Your Message,'* you are saying loudly:

- ✓ **Why** people should **buy** your products, produce or service!
- ✓ **Why** your products, produce or services is **better** than others on the market!
- ✓ **Why** your products, produce or services are **different** than any others in the market place.

> *1. Why people should **buy** your products, produce or service?*

When you are selling anything in the market place you need to identify your *'Point of Difference'* early. You need to be strong about 'Why' people should **buy** your product, produce or service.

Mary can identify the health benefits of her dark chocolate. She can say with confidence: *'eat in moderation and enjoy the benefits of a delicious treat'.*

She can list the locally grown ingredients used which, in turn, become a benefit to the customer or consumer.

Joe can expand his message to say, *'healthy eating leads to healthy living'* or establish his cakes and biscuits in the minds' of his customers to say, *'when eaten in moderation, these are **body friendly foods'** and add, 'These food are high in complex carbohydrates'.* Then expand his message on the value of the food – complex carbohydrate are important to the

- ✓ Body
- ✓ Brain and
- ✓ Overall wellbeing to the person. This 'body friendly' food gives 'life energy and more'.

Because '...the market is the market,' you need to look and study every word you write down when it's going into the public arena.

Crafting Your Message takes time, but its invaluable time spent and will help you to sell your products, produce or services more efficiently.

Crafting Your Message means being succinct and *'Does What It Says It Does On The Can!'*

2. Why your products, produce or services is **better** than others on the market!

If your product, produce or services is better than others in the market place, why aren't you saying so?

Mary knows her chocolates are *'delicious'* and she can honestly say that*: 'these chocolates are delicious'.* Her customers have told her they are*, 'Delicious'.*

Joe knows his biscuits and cakes are made of only the best local ingredients he can buy and Nigel knows his tomatoes are good because his business is genuinely and continually expanding.

The '**Difference'** of your product, produce or services is your **defining** mark in the market place

What is the **'Difference'** of the three above products, how can Joe, Mary and Nigel tell the market place about their difference?

In the above three case studies, each person will be able to immediately speak of their 'Point Of Difference' and say:

> ➢ Why people should **buy** their product, produce or services,

> Why their products, produce or services are **better,**
> Why their product, produce or services are **different**'.

When you *'Craft Your Message,'* you are 'drilling down' deeply into your thinking and you are evaluating your worth, the worth of your product, produce or services and what it means to you.

You are looking at:

- ✓ Your personal values
- ✓ The values you hold for the selling you are doing
- ✓ Your personal esteem
- ✓ Your personal identity
- ✓ The personal growth you are creating for yourself and
- ✓ What you are selling for now and your future.

You have a lot at stake so you might as well get it right in the first instance.

When you get into the habit of *'Crafting Your Message'* you are taking responsibility of the words you speak and write about the product, produce or services you are selling. You are not handing over your responsibility for your selling position.

You are stating:

- ✓ I want to know more about this;

- ✓ I can give more information when I know more about this;
- ✓ I become more effective when I know the techniques of how to 'Craft My Message' and the 'Words Within My Message;'
- ✓ I am empowered when I know the words I speak about my product, produce or services;
- ✓ What I'm selling is of value and has benefits for my customers, clients or the consumers I speak to.

When people feel empowerment in selling they become inspirational to other people in the market place. Empowerment has positive energy entwined within the words spoken and written and makes winners.

The Internet, The Worldwide, Web (www)

It is without a doubt the fastest growing device for contacting and working with people all over the world.

We are in the *'Information Age' and this age* is all about Communication. *'Crafting Your Message'* is but one small, but vitally important tool, you need to use.

The internet allows many people to go into business and to sell more and more products, produce, even services on line.

If you haven't got computer skills, you need to gain these valuable assets. You need to know how the world, wide web (www) works.

Even working within your local community, you can gain many orders by having a cost effective website built. People automatically, these days, want a web address. They size you up while talking to you. They want to look at your website before buying from you or making contact with you.

My Sales Director has said, '….while I'm speaking to people on the phone about the courses we run, I can hear them (the contact) clicking through the computer looking for the website'.

There's more about the internet later in the book.

The general public is more 'savvy' about market competition and will only buy from you if:

- ✓ There is a benefit for them, their partner or family?
- ✓ The customer, client in the 21st Century will first and nearly always ask: 'What's In It For Me?'
- ✓ They feel they can trust you!
- ✓ You can deliver what you say you can deliver!
- ✓ If 'it's too hard,' they, the customer or consumer, doesn't understand what you are saying or selling; they will instantly walk away or if in a phone conversation, put

- down the phone and disengage from the interaction or communication taking place!
- ✓ They, the consumer or customer, want instant reaction, positive outcomes or they demand their money back.

You Always Stand To Make Good (A Bad, Negative Customer, Consumer Experience) When A Refund Policy Or Guarantee Is In Place.

- ✓ When you are honest - if there is a breakdown in communication, or if the product, produce or services doesn't live up to their (the consumer or customer's expectations). If, you have an unhappy customer or client, you can endorse satisfaction by having **a refund policy or guarantee in place.**

Understanding Target Marketing & Crafting Your Message

Keeping Your Customers or Clients – many businesses become established and forget about the current or past customers, consumers or the consumers they have. The **dormant** customer or consumer may be a customer you first made contact with, but through time, the person has been overlooked.

Making contact with your customers, clients or consumers' on a monthly basis is a way of keeping your people interested and happy in what you are selling. With the internet, there are many devices you can use to make regular contact with people.

Newsletters

Newsletters, to begin with, need to be only one page and can be sent out to thousands of people regularly, once every two weeks, monthly or by-monthly. You can write longer newsletters as you progress and really expand on the story you want to tell.

The sample newsletter below, is just that - a sample. You can make many changes and adapt or use this one as your base newsletter.

Some marketing people like to send out long newsletters involving many pages of writing – this may work with some products, produce or services. Again, you will need to test, register and record the interaction and reaction which takes place.

There is a national move for people to become closer and to feel they belong to different organizations, events or communities in the 21st Century. In sales, you are in the perfect position to draw people together and there is no better tool than the newsletter, so use it. Take advantage of this powerful medium but use it with discretion and integrity.

The newsletter will allow you:

- ✓ Invite people to events or gatherings

- ✓ Advertise your latest products
- ✓ Tell people about the fund raising event the business is supporting
- ✓ Run raffles
- ✓ Offer larger prizes for competitions
- ✓ Run children's events
- ✓ Have a Seniors' Day
- ✓ Have a 'Is It Your Birthday Today?' celebration and more - you would need to think 'Outside Of The Box' to get your thoughts working and adapt your newsletter to your business or selling structure.

Using Mary's example newsletter, below, read it again and think of a way you can adapt it to meet your needs.

Heavenly Chocolates

Newsletter 2 March 2012

Welcome to our regular Newsletter.

It's nearly Easter and it's time to revive that 'Old Favourite' the Banana Split. We are making some differences to the Banana Split by using Banana and Ginger Ganache in a rich dark chocolate sauce and fresh cherries.

Delicious samples will be available for three days only from Monday 4th April to Wednesday 6th April at

At Chocolatiere,
'Chocolate Indulgence,' The Village, Hempshire

We know our customers are going to enjoy this new sensory taste, so please join us.

If you cannot join us on the above dates, please tear off the slip below and bring it into *'Chocolate Indulgence,'* so we can share this exciting new taste with you.

Dear *'Chocolate Indulgence,'*

Please give to our valued customer, two Ginger and Banana chocolates.

Valued during April 2017.

Thank you for your support.

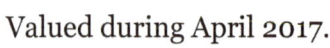

Advertising

Newspaper advertising can be a 'shot in the dark' if you do not *'Craft Your Message'*.

Other Ventures

If you are starting up a florist shop or working in a creative business, you can begin working and starting from home. You can test your market place. Start small and test, test and test.

(Warning, not all businesses can be started at home. If you don't own the property, you will need to check your lease, covenant or council planning regulations.)

If you go ahead with your ideas, or you are in a newly established selling role, you need to target particular groups. The obvious groups within the flower trade are:

- Bereavements
- Weddings
- Corporate Functions
- Birthdays and
- Births

One area which is missed by many people working within the flower industry is the Corporate Employer who wants to keep his staff happy. By putting an advertisement in a business magazine or in the local newspaper's Business Section saying,

> **Are You Busy?**
>
> 'Are you a busy Corporate Employer and do you value your staff? Do you want to keep your staff because staff changes cost money (big money), disrupts work flow and interrupt your business? If so, you need this. Don't worry, we can take care of those special days in the lives of your staff by sending the right flowers for the right occasion: PA's day, Birthdays, Anniversaries or Celebration Days. Join today, our **'Don't Forget Club'**.
>
> We guarantee to remind you of every Special Date during the year when you join the 'Don't Forget Club'. As appreciation of your joining, we will send a free bouquet of freshly cut flowers, valued at $50.00 to the person of your choice. Just Contact Julie at **'Blossoms For Ever'** on: 000 777 777. For details of my free recorded message: 000 blossom.

This type of advertising is 'Lead Generation' and such text, with changed content can be applied to most businesses, such as:

- ✓ Restaurants
- ✓ Chocolate Shop Outlets
- ✓ Florists
- ✓ Perfumery And Accessory Outlets or
- ✓ Gift Outlets
- ✓ Department Stores

It's powerful, targeted and direct advertising.

Advertising needs to be compelling and give to the reader the message he or she wants to read – a message which meets their needs.

Effective Advertising Includes:

Identifying The Problem Or Aggravate The Problem And Offer A Solution

➢ Find The Problem/s – it's always the problem that needs solving!

Here you identify a 'problem' – if there wasn't a problem there wouldn't be a need! When people have a problem they need to find a solution!

Effective advertising highlights a problem, aggravates the situation and then offers a solution.

In order for people to face or identify a problem, there will need to be some arousal, aggravation or disturbance which brings the problem to the surface. Julie, the florist has identified a problem in the above advertisement:

✓ ***Identify The Problem:*** *'Corporate employer who wants to keep his good staff and keep them happy!'*

✓ ***Arousal, Aggravation, Disturbance Identifying The Problems:*** *'…changes cost money (big money), disrupts work flow and interrupts your business?'*

✓ ***Solution:*** *We guarantee to remind you of every Special Date during the year when you join the **'Don't Forget Club'**.*

It takes some practice to create leading advertisements – the sample above is an 'easy to relate to' formula and if followed, will assist you on the road to successful 'copy' writing.

Crafted Messages Need To Tell The Story

- ✓ What Are You Saying In The Market Place?
- ✓ What Is Interesting About You In The Market Place?
- ✓ Why You Are Attractive To The Market Place?

With *Crafted Messages*, you need to link your message to the 'needs' and 'wants' of the client, customer or consumers'.

Your Unique Selling Proposition (USP)

Creating a Unique Selling Proposition takes thought and work.

Overview

Michael had been in his tile and carpet business for the last fifteen years. His premises were looking old and tired and the big DIY businesses were taking a big part of his trade.

The Story

At first, Michael saw his weekly figures go down and was confident that eventually his old customers' would return.

Michael's hopes were being quickly eroded away by the weekly numbers coming from his cash register readings and knew, '…..*for the time of year, there are not the same number of weekend customers as there were in the previous years!*'

Michael did some serious thinking, read a few books and decided to close his store for two weeks while he did a major revamp.

The store had been overcrowded, dark, full of shadowy corners, dingy and messy with no easy format for his customers to find what they wanted or needed to buy.

Michael, had earlier in the year, consulted some experts who suggested certain changes. One suggestion, though simple, Michael had previously overlooked:

- ✓ *'Change the word from store to showroom'* and the second suggestion
- ✓ Create one large display area that was light, sharp, tasteful but intensely colourful'.

Michael set about making his business transformation. By doing what had been suggested, it meant knocking down heavy brick interior walls. The walls were replaced by 'slip track' runners where customers could easily flick through displays of floor tiles. With each tile display, examples of sharp, up to the minute, interior, patio and exterior designs were displayed through using videos and glossy brochures.

In the carpet section of the showroom, Michael had displayed locally made European and British, luxury carpets through to cheaper harder wearing, European and British carpets for family and games' rooms.

Michael's commitment to buying from the local European market, rather than cheaper imported products, was a gamble!

His showroom was in an established area of Berkshire, England and he was prepared to take the risk of staying European!

The showroom was finished and was looking sheik and extremely smart. On the day of the opening Michael had organised a 'Grand Re-Opening' and had invited as many media people as possible. He had also invited all of his customers (old and new). Knowing that most of his business takes place at the weekend, he made sure the re-opening was going to take place on Saturday at 12.00 noon.

Michael had a message to send to the public and put a small advertisement in the local paper and magazines.

He knew a bit about creating the Unique Selling Point (USP) in marketing and needed to use his skills to re-establish his business.

Michael had previously had a very good business but with the onset of fierce competition from the DIY giants and the importing of Asian products, the market was becoming harder and harder to penetrate.

Michael had two choices: close the business or re-establish the business with a higher, sleek, sophisticated and up-to-date profile. The latter prevailed.

The up-to-date profile would allow him to be considered, by his customer base, to be the first point of contact before they went looking at the country-wide DIY stores.

His newspaper advertisement was:

Grand Re-Opening
Michael's Interior Showroom

We Welcome All of Our Existing and New Customers To Our Grand Re-Opening of

Michael's Interior Showroom

Saturday 18th August.

12.00 Noon

All Purchases Made During Our Opening Will Receive A 20% Discount

Our New Showroom Displays:

- A range of exclusive Italian and British manufactured tiles
- Scottish & European woven luxury carpets &
- New ranges of family, durable British carpets
- Solid wood, custom designed furniture
- Soft furnishings from silk cushions to stylish mirrors,
- Taps & Bathroom fittings of distinction &
- Custom Made Kitchens

Corner Ways, The Green, Hinchcombe
When You Join Us On Saturday Between The Hours
Of 12.00 & 4.00pm
We Will Give You Two Silk Cushions &
You Can Join the Draw **For $2,000** Off The Value Of Your New Kitchen

---

With any form of advertising, there needs to be benefits and features for the customer or consumer. Michael is offering a number of features but he is also offering the uniqueness of his products and the service he is providing.

He is out to re-capture his share of the market. He wants to regain his old customer base and has thought about the long-term sales and business structure.

He is offering specific items; he is specific in his advertising, promotions, selling power and knows what he is talking about. Plus, Michael is offering a new experience to his customers in the refurbishment, stylish and comfortable shopping environment.

Michael could take his ideas further. He can offer an *'End Of Financial Year'* Sale. He could offer last year's products at:

'50% Off – Everything Must Go!'

Through the *'End Of Financial Year Sale,'* he is keeping his cash flow moving and making room for his latest stock. The benefits of his actions are:

- ✓ Income stimulation
- ✓ Old stock removal
- ✓ Excitement in the community – everybody loves a sale!
- ✓ Community togetherness
- ✓ People love the latest fashion item
- ✓ Have 'nibbles' and maybe a single glass of champagne!

✓ Make it an event to remember – hire a celebrity to 'kick start the sale'.

The Unique Selling Proposition (USP) Can Happen With Every Sale Once You Know The Tools To Use.

1 Each advertisement is unique – it must lead the customer to think about changing their mind about the item they are considering buying. Reeves (1961) identified: 'Buy this product, and you will get *this specific benefit*'.

2 The USP is an offer that the competition does not offer and cannot offer within its particular field of advertising. The USP offers something the customer 'Wants,' therefore the strength in the *Crafted Message* must be strong enough to change established thinking and habits.

3 The USP is strong and clearly explains enough about the product, produce or service to move thousands or millions of people from buying with their old habits at established outlets and to re-establish their buying habits to newly promoted products, produce and services at new outlets.

Michael is after his share of the market place and knows he has previously had a strong market base. However, changing times, changing attitudes, changing buying habits and the free-market economies of the world are opening up more competition. Many cheaper, not necessarily inferior imported products are exported globally - this adds to the *'Lion's Share Of The Market Place'.*

Michael also knows, he must be sharper in his thinking and actions; he cannot become complacent with his business and allow the business to run itself in the future!

Now, identify your (USP).

In this Chapter we've covered two essential areas of Selling:

- ✓ *Crafting Your Message &*
- ✓ *The Unique Selling Proposition (USP).*

Both areas are interesting – you may need to re-read the chapter a number of times before you fully understand the important role they play in Selling

YOUR NOTES

Chapter Five

Radio, Television Advertising And The Worldwide Web (www)

To become totally dependent on radio or television advertising is a big mistake.

With all money spent on advertising, selling or marketing there needs to be a *'return value'*. A *'return value'* is the number of sales taking place and adds momentum to your income.

Radio and Television advertising are valuable in some instances. Radio and television advertising are a benefit if you have an event or function and you want to announce it. It's impossible to announce in a ten, twenty or thirty second advertisement, your total (USP) message, but it is possible to drive an announcement by saying:

> *'Save 20% at Michael's Interior Showroom Grand Re-Opening, Saturday 18th August, Hinchcombe'.*

> Or

> *'Grand Re-Opening, Saturday 18th August,'* Save 20% at Michael's Interior Showroom, Hinchcombe'.

Short radio and television advertising <u>*does not allow you to create a USP.*</u> However, radio and television announcements can be used effectively to advertise the advertisement!

Going a little deeper, if you have an existing advertisement in say, the Yellow Pages, you can make that advertisement work and deliver great responses through using radio or television. This medium can be used to drive your existing advertisement to your website.

If for instance, you have a privately owned and independent school for dancing, art or general education, you can use radio and television advertising effectively by saying:

>'Do you care about education, then go to www.careeducation@springfield.com'

Another instance maybe for a local panel beater:

>'There's 3 Reasons why you should go to Page 205 of the Yellow Pages for Dan's Panel Beating
>- Good Job done
>- Speedy repairs
>- Cost effective & Saves You Money'.

Or, you could say:

>'Worried About that car dent, then go to: www.danspanelbeating.com'

Or,

> *'Car dent, not a worry, at www.danspanelbeating.com'*

This is short, sharp and to the point advertising and can be extremely cost effective.

Rivers Clothing and Shoe Outlets in Queensland Australia, blitz the television screen with short, sharp ads. Recently, they have been showing winter boots, no words spoken, just the boots worn on real, human legs wearing winter boots, walking in imitation snow – the legs turning the boots in about three different directions – there are no human heads or bodies showing, just boots and the written words:

> 'For three days only $15.00'

This appears on each design of boot.

(The power of advertising is in the words spoken or written and the picture created.)

Word Of Mouth Advertising

The people of Queensland will spread the word organically for Rivers by saying to another person:

> *'Did you see, Rivers have boots for just $15.00?'*

When advertising 'self-generates' like the above example, the word becomes infectious or contagious.

Taking 'Word of Mouth' television advertising a little deeper and going back to the school example: using three, 'still' and clear but detailed photographs including:

1. students' work or students being taught in the classroom
2. a good external building shot and
3. front notice board showing the web address:
4. *www.careeducation@springfield.com*

The strong visual combination of pictures can send a powerful message by saying,

'We Care, At Care Education'.

Background music also adds to the effectiveness of the advertising – it gives an ambiance to the overall message.

Such advertising is powerful, effective and gives results.

Advertising needs to be:

- ✓ *Appealing* – it has an 'emotional pull' to those people seeing or hearing it
- ✓ *Attractive* – it must be pleasing to the eye, have colour and be in focus – 'a picture speaks a thousand words'

- ✓ *Legitimate* – it does what it says it does. The boots are good value, even if only worn for one season, at $15.00
- ✓ *Achieving* - the students' in the 'Care Education Program' are meeting all expectations in academic achievement and the advertising needs to contain:
- ✓ *Honesty* – the advertising does exactly what it claims to do, it may also be
- ✓ *Aggravating* –Aggravating advertising can make the audience look twice, even make them chuckle; this form of advertising may be short-lived as it contains an annoyance factor.

With all advertising you are asking people to buy from you. You are asking people to change the way:

- ➤ They think
- ➤ The way they buy
- ➤ The attitude they have
- ➤ The habits they have, and
- ➤ The actions they take and the
- ➤ Lifestyle they live

To get people to 'change' is the most difficult of any human behaviour to achieve. People will only change their behaviour and buy from you if you have a worthwhile message or story to tell.

They will not buy long-term if you do not meet their expectations in the first instance. Consumer demands can be fickle if they are left feeling dissatisfied.

Website Based Businesses And Selling

I too, have developed many websites in conjunction with web designers. I've had designers create, creative and different websites! They look attractive and effective but, in reality, they do nothing. They do nothing because they do not represent what the greater public are looking for.

With website design, you need the website to be so effective, that it almost instantly gives the reader, your potential customer, the information they are looking for.

When a person Googles for information, they are interested in buying goods or items on-line and usually want things to happen in a hurry. People want sound and honest information about the item they want to buy; they are looking for effective, easy to use websites.

If a website becomes a hurdle or is too hard to use, you will lose customers, potential long-term clients' and collect unhappy people in a hurry.
After spending a great deal of money and many years of working with websites, we have found a *'touch of magic'* that will help businesses connect their advertising to their websites.

If, however, you have chosen your business name already, this *'gem of magic'* may be difficult for you to adapt.

We have found, if you:

> Go to 'Google Ad Words,' key in the words you are interested in – words which you feel represent what you are selling in goods or information about the services you offer. These words are also directly linked to your business ideas or names. See what is the Highest, not so High or Medium string of words being keyed into the Ad Words that possibly relate to your goods or service.
>
> (Ad Words are those words which people key into Google when they are looking to buy or for information about products, produce or services; keying in this information may come from different people working with their computers around the world!)
> The Ad Words have numbers recorded to strings of words, you are looking for strings of words - the strings of words are recorded on the left-hand side of the screen.
>
> Once in the 'Ad Words Table' – you need to record the information you are looking at and for. This information is in the number of searches being done against the string of words you have typed in.

(Google records popular strings of words and the strings are numbered this gives the Ad Words their ratings.)

How do the string of words you've typed in relate to the Google strings of words?

You need to look at the big numbers and see how they are rating in the Ad Words; if for instance, you have typed in 'chocolates on line,' (at the time of writing this book, we found there were 600,000 people looking at *'chocolates on line'.*) You need to look at the numbers which represent 'Medium'. Medium numbers in this example would be about of 300,000 or even less!

You will need to identify the string of words you want to use and how these relate to the numbers in the Ad Words! By doing this, you can identify a mid-range. To give you an example:

Think of a string of words which will identify your product, produce or service or identify your business. You may not see a matching string in Google Ad Words, so type the words in, you think will fit your business or sales.

Using Mary as an example again, Mary has typed in: *heavenly chocolates,* this isn't proving successful.

However, if Mary keys in: *'gifts of chocolate,'* the monthly contact rate, (at the time of writing this book) is 49,500. This records as 'Medium' and would make a good start. Mary can keep searching, this time she keys in:

'chocolate for chocolate making' which measures 'Medium' and records a monthly contact number of 90,500. Does this name help Mary? Not really at this time, not unless she changes her business name! Not a good idea as her business has started to grow and people already know her as *'Heavenly Chocolates'.*

Ideally, first, before doing anything and if you want your website to register highly on Google, you need to find a name which is going to fit your product, produce or service and your business image.

Mary, thinks for a while and has another go; she could use the words: *'gifts of chocolate'.*

Searching on a domain name website, Mary Keys in *gifts of chocolate and the name is available as dot com, dot au, dot org, dot net and so on*.

Mary then keys into the domain name site: *heavenlygiftsofchocolates,* and that name is also available as a domain name, but it's not going to be strong enough for Google Ad Words because it has the name: 'heavenly' at the beginning of the string. If this string is not registering on Google Ad Words, it will not drive people to Mary's website.

Mary now knows, if she looks for a string in Google Ad Words, she will get a better idea of the names to use in her Domain Name.

If Mary had known about Google Ad Words before naming her business, she could have called the business: *'Gifts of Chocolates'*. She would have married up her:

- Registered business name
- Her registered ABN number or equivalent, and
- Her Domain Name.
- All would have matched with Google Ad Words.

If you are an on-line business, you need to consider all of the above.

Matching the:

- Domain name, to Google Ad Words and
- Matching the registered business name to the domain name – these are vitally important in on-line selling in the 21st Century.

Mary can still trade as: *Heavenly Gifts of Chocolate* in her brand name, but she would be wise to register it as a second business name.

Domain names and Google Ad Words are not difficult to use; you need to become familiar with the Google Ad Word website because it is an extremely powerful tool.

If you want to make your business work, you need to have all your efforts working together and working and taking you in one direction:

- ✓ Making sales happen
- ✓ Making the efforts you put into selling work for you.

When you are setting up a business or going into the role of selling, there are many areas that you need to become familiar with. These areas are not always covered by conventional education or by your previous experiences.

If you become aware of situations before they arise, you will be forewarned!

The web is continually growing and developing and can be a minefield when you first start delving into how it works.

Working with your business and the web effectively will pay dividends – it will be where most shopping is done in the future, so it's better to start early and 'get in before the rush!'

Effective 'on-line shopping' will open up many areas of the market place for you, but you must operate effectively.

Many councils and education and community groups are now offering training in e-commerce.

Many areas have been covered in this chapter from advertising on local television to taking you on a trip to Google Ad Words.

In our business, we use all the tools and devices I write about.

The web is a powerful tool when you are selling – with a bit of knowledge, it has made many people extremely wealthy.

YOUR NOTES

Chapter Six

Communication And Information In The 21st Century

Communication is not as simple as it looks. Communication is about giving to other people information which contains a message!

Within most received messages, there is a form of *'Action'* to be taken by the receiver.

In psychology, we know that an *'Action'* is a response to a message sent from the brain area of one person to another person. The person receiving the information is known as a receiver.

Most messages contain the information: 'translation' and 'response'. The response means 'take action: – *I'm waiting for an answer from you'.*

Psychologists relate to 'translation' of information, when 'response' is the intended outcome, is an *'Action Potential'.*

'Action Potential' is a movement or movements made by you as the response to a stimulus you have received through your senses:

- ✓ Hearing
- ✓ Seeing

- ✓ Smelling
- ✓ Touching or
- ✓ Tasting

When *receiving* a message, it may be through one or many of your senses working together.

The message is sent from a sense or your senses and travels throughout your body through an electronic message which is sent to your brain. Your senses are the 'Point of Entry' for the messages sent to you from other people or from situations which are happening in your environment.

If, for instance, you see a road accident while you are driving down the motorway. Your eyes, (your visual sense) send a message to your brain - this message is received at (*Reception*), translated (*Translation*) takes place by your mind which sends a message back to your hands and feet: *'keep the car steady, slow down, stop and help if you are needed!'*

This message from your mind is your *'Action Potential'.* Your *'Action Potential'* may be to keep driving and say to you: 'don't be a sticky beak' or 'pull over and give a hand!'

To reinforce this idea: in computer terms, your brain is your hardware that houses your mind, for simplicity sake, I will call your mind: the software for your brain.

With the analogy above and the car accident, once the information goes from the brain to the mind, within the '*Translation*' - your mind wants to make sense of the information it has received.

This information is valued for its worth and immediate and possible action or for: good, bad, or rubbish, or it may be of value sometime in the future! It's either stored away or not thought about again – simply, thrown out; you know this, because you have little to no recollection of it!

Once this process has taken place, the remainder of the message is transferred back to your limbs, or senses and a response takes place: 'smell the rose,' 'feel the skin cream,' 'kick a ball,' 'pay a bill,' 'cook some food,' 'pick the children up from school,' 'do the washing' and so on. It takes many thousands of these small messages, received from your senses, to perform one simple task such as: blow your nose!

For more information, about selling, please go to: www. www.booksforreadingonline.com and buy '*Discovery Your Selling Power*'.

In all selling or buying, from working in the 'Pit' of the 'stock market,' to serving an ice cream at an ice creamery, each and every person receives information in a similar way.

In a selling situation, it's how you internalize the incoming information to the 'action,' 're-action' or the 'Action Potential' you select to use that makes the difference to how you sell.

Reciprocal Communication

Reciprocal communication happens when you are sending out a message - you hope the message is received as a positive piece of information by the receiver.

Vast numbers, too many to be quantifiable, of these messages are transmitted each and every day in the selling world alone. Transmission of messages is sent by the transmitter, you, and received by a receiver, usually your customer, client or potential client.

Because of the complexity of language, messages can become jumbled, mixed up and misunderstood.

The complexity of the communication you send out includes:

- your character
- your personality

- your home environment
- your work environment and its culture
- the groups of people you mix with
- the groups you have mixed with in the past
- your home sub-culture
- the sub-culture of your community and
- the national culture of your country.

In each and every piece of information you send out, it will include fragments of each culture and sub-culture you have interacted with, lived or worked with, all of this, is indeed, you. This all contributes to the person you are today!

Without going too deeply into personality, it's the different combinations or the parts of your personality you use when you want to make sales happen. By using your positive personality, you can make yourself a winning seller.

Your positive personality allows you to interact with other people. Within your personality, you have a judgment or balancing mechanism which guides you to see, listen and feel the communication taking place.

Reciprocal information allows sales to happen or take place. Reciprocal information is the pattern or blueprint of the words you are working with when giving and receiving information.

Reciprocal information means the information between you and your customer, client or consumer is working effectively - you are both thinking and talking with the same message.

Reciprocal information is paramount in selling.

Effective reciprocal information has the power to:

- ✓ Inform
- ✓ Persuade
- ✓ Entertain
- ✓ Move
- ✓ Motivate
- ✓ Change
- ✓ Enthuse
- ✓ Stimulate and
- ✓ Re-generate other people and these skills contribute to the selling techniques needed by every person who is selling for a living.

Reciprocal Communication is balanced, positive and emotionally charged information which allows communities, states and countries to work effectively together.

The Five Steps In Reciprocal Communication Are:

   1. *Creation*
   2. *Transmission*
   3. *Reception*
   4. *Translation and*
   5. *Response*

1)   Creation

A thought leads to the beginning of an idea and many ideas come together to support the creation of the message. Many messages are transmitted daily in all forms of selling. People may be thinking:

- ❖ '…how many units will I sell today?'
- ❖ '…if I sell more of those today, it will help me pay for so and so!'
- ❖ I need to sell more, so that I can get that bonus to pay the back rent!'
- ❖ 'It would be good if we could 'clear the decks and sell that old stock to make room for the new stock arriving next week!'
- ❖ 'I need to get this brief written up so that it's ready for the Court Hearing on Monday…' This is the creation of the messages in response or added to the brief

and the messages must be ready by Monday!

❖ If it's not ready by Monday, he or she may find they don't have a job at the end of the month – they are therefore selling their time, knowledge, expertise and effort to have their work completed on time.

So many thoughts and so much to do - the human mind is constantly processing information. It takes small pieces of information in the shape of thoughts and blends thoughts together allowing ideas to be born.

2) Transmission

The transmission of information in selling needs to be:

- ✓ Clear
- ✓ Un-fragmented
- ✓ Without interference
- ✓ Stable
- ✓ Have a 'genuine story' attached – *every item on the supermarket shelf has a story attached to it; so it's your job to find the story connected to the item you are selling!*
- ✓ Be worthwhile to the receiver, and
- ✓ A benefit to the receiver.

3)   Reception

When you send out a message, you want to know the receiver has received the 'correct' message - this is the *'Reception Of The Message'*. When a message is sent out and it's either jumbled or incorrect, it will be received at the *'Reception'* as jumbled or incorrect.

This is why you need to make sure the message is:

- ✓ Understandable
- ✓ Unambiguous and definite
- ✓ Uninhibited by other contaminating messages and
- ✓ Understood by the person you are sending your information to.

4)   Translation

It's in the *'Translation'* that messages can be contaminated. If your message isn't clearly sent out, your customer, client or consumers will translate your information incorrectly.

Your message needs to be without any ambiguity; your customers need to know clearly that your message is going to meet their: 'needs' and 'wants'. If this is not so, you will have a problem in selling.

'Translation' are your customers, clients or consumers asking:

- Is this of benefit to me?
- Can I use this information?
- Is this the information I'm looking for?
- Will this information help me get to the next step?
- Do I need this information at this time? And
- How is this information relevant to me?

You can see why your transference of information has to be crystal clear. Crystal clear transmitting of the information only comes about when you are thinking clearly.

Selling is about sending out *'Crystal-Clear'* messages.

5) Response

We all wait to see what the response will be when we send out a message. From sending out a letter to a friend, having a bet on a horse at the races, whether or not you've made that sale?

Response carries a *'passage of time'* and is only part of the bigger picture. It takes many responses to form the bigger picture when you are selling. Responses happen when negotiations are under way and the *journey* of selling is in progress.

Very few sales happen without going through some form of *'passage of time'*. There are various lengths in the *'passage of time'* in the selling process; it varies from the item or object/s being sold. From selling real estate to selling a pair of shoes or selling:

- A house
- An expensive leather jacket
- A lipstick
- Packet of biscuits
- The latest up-market sports car
- The development of a software package for a large hospital, to selling your
- Produce at the Sunday markets.

The *Response* carries with it the building blocks of the selling process; each building block has its own unique DNA and, as a seller, you need to understand how your 'Building Blocks' are working!

Not often mentioned in the Selling Process is **'The Game Of Selling'.**

Every sale you have is part of the 'Game of Selling'. Selling is fun and exciting. When you are selling, you are working with parts of your human psyche and it's that part of your personality that brings out the challenge to 'win' and the 'winner' within you.

The challenge of selling is to make as many sales as possible, the more sales you make, the more you become a winner and the richer you become, not only in money value but in expertise value!

We all feel good when we win something and selling is no different.

When you sell something, especially if you have been putting down many 'Building Blocks' over a number of months or even years, to see a positive end result is rewarding, stimulating and satisfying.

Body Language

Body language is the use of non-verbal communication, which includes:

- ✓ the use of body posture
- ✓ facial expression
- ✓ eye movements

- ✓ gestures from limb movement, for example: offer your hand, kick the imaginary ball.

These are all forms of communication.

Body language is the ability to use your mental and physical ability to send information to another person. It's the ability to make contact with other people, through body signals which can be done, even subconsciously.

Negative Body Language Can:

- ➢ Destroy A Business
- ➢ Reduce Customer Demand
- ➢ Give A Bad Reputation
- ➢ Reduce The Bottom Line
- ➢ Add To Stress In The Work Place
- ➢ Reduce Sales Which
- ➢ Reduces The Cash Flow

Positive Body Language Can:

- ✓ Enhance Business Image
- ✓ Brings In The Customers
- ✓ Increase Cash Flow
- ✓ Increase The Bottom Line
- ✓ Add To A Positive Work Place Environment

- ✓ Increase In Business And Personal Achievements And
- ✓ Increase In Work Place Satisfaction.

We have discussed the process the mind goes through when goods and services are sold in the marketplace.

One area that is often overlooked is the body language of the seller.

Overview

I have already said, *'a picture speaks a thousand words'.*

Recently, on a quick trip back to England, my husband and I went into an exclusive chocolate shop to buy some hand-made chocolates.

Over many years, I have spent a lot of money in this chocolate shop and have always enjoyed the experience of seeing the beautifully made chocolates and speaking to the friendly staff.

However, the last time I went into the shop, will possibly be the last time I will ever buy from that shop.

The Story

The woman behind the counter was a challenge. There was little to no expression in her face and as I watched on, while waiting in the line to be served, she was treating every customer with the same contempt. The contempt for the customer was at the point of bland but total rudeness.

She knew little to nothing about the chocolates she was selling, her body language was telling me about how she was thinking when serving the people in front of me: 'you're too much of an effort to serve'. There was no 'Hello,' or 'Hello, how are you today?' or 'Can I help you?' or 'Thank you,' or 'Enjoy your chocolates'. Absolutely nothing in conversation or softness in her actions or mannerisms, it is after all, a chocolate shop and usually a happy and self-indulgent place to be!

By the time we had all of our chocolates together, there was a considerable amount of money sitting in the basket waiting to be totaled and paid.

Exasperated, I watched as the woman took the chocolates from the basket and keyed the sum amounts into the cash register. At the end of the total and as she gave me the change from a fifty pound note, without any warmth in her emotion or expression in her face or pleasure in handing me over a considerable sized bag of different boxed chocolates, I had to say something.

Again, infuriated, I said, 'Are you always so rude, is this job too much of an effort for you, if you don't like what you are doing, you should find another job!' I was so annoyed I couldn't wait to get out of that shop, never to return.

It's as easy to be nice to people as it is to be miserable. In fact, it takes more life-energy to be miserable than happy. Being miserable shortens your life span, adds to illness, makes the days you live harder to work with and loses you masses of friends; there are little to no advantages in being rude or miserable!

This happens time and time again in selling situations. If you are employed to sell, that is what you do: you sell and make it something even better than it is.

You make it a challenge to do better than you did the day, week or year before. Every bit of effort put into selling has its rewards.

Your body language is a powerful tool and like your mind, you have the choice to use it to be totally destructive to yourself and the organization you are working for or use it and take the absolute advantages it offers. After all, a smile costs you nothing and you get bucket loads of good cheer back, even monstrous sales in return.

In this chapter, I have covered how your mind and body language can be used to make sales work for you.

The simple knowledge of knowing how your body language can interfere with gaining good and large sales should alert you if your sales have been poor or slumping.

You may need to check how you are 'Translating' your information and the messages you are sending out through your body language!

YOUR NOTES

Chapter Seven

Selling Is An Ancient Custom

Trading started in pre-historic times when people realized they could communicate with each other. Communication allowed people to trade and therefore gain more in the goods and services they needed.

Communication allowed people to work and socialize together; when socializing takes place, people can gain more in the goods or services they need, which in turn, allows their lives to be lived more comfortably.

Selling and buying (known as trade) is an ancient custom. The activity of trading could reach back to more than one hundred and fifty thousand years or earlier. There is evidence of the first market taking place at least fifty thousand years ago.

Prior to the introduction of coins, bartering was the preferred way of transaction. With bartering for goods and services it is difficult to establish a true 'worth' or 'value' for either the goods or service being transacted.

Trading and establishing a *'worth'* or *'value'* for the products, produce or services being traded has been a contentious part of commerce for centuries. To secure a 'value of worth' for goods or services, gold was first used as a 'value' tool and measured against goods, grains, livestock, linens, silks and possibly spices.

Croesus, a Lydian King (635 BC) is credited with issuing the first true gold coins.

The original Lydian coins were made from electrum, an alloy which is a combination of gold and silver combined with other minerals; these were the first coins minted.

The electrum money system was flawed: merchants, in the market place, did not know the 'true value' of the coins they were trading with, so they could not accurately value products, produce or any other tradable item for its true 'value of worth'.

This dilemma came about because of the varying combinations of gold and silver used in minting the coins. If for instance a coin contained more silver, it's was considered to be a low value metal. Gold, however, was considered to be a high value metal.

The conflicting value of the coins caused arguments and tension between the merchants in the market place.

The matter was brought to the attention of the King. King Croesus had a solution, the. King was not only extremely rich King but he was also intelligent enough to know that there needs to be an 'accepted standard' which measures a purity in the exchange of money for goods and services bought and sold.

The currency of coins needed to be standardized.

King Croesus developed the first technology of a metal extraction process dividing the gold from the silver.

With this technology in place, and pure gold coins used for their currency, the Lydian merchants knew they were trading with pure gold minted coins. The pure gold of the coins became the 'true measure' used in commerce during that time.

Gold, because of its perceived intrinsic value, and as a commodity has been used to measure individual wealth, the worth of countries and nations.

Gold commodities, along with other commodities such as iron ore, mining, other minerals, spices and grains are used as the 'backbone'. of trading; this has been since human beings understood the value of the assets they own, want or can steal.

As the centuries progressed, gold coins proved to be too heavy to take on international trading routes and to the international markets. Another problem developed: that of theft while the merchants were on their journey to trade.

'Promissory Notes' rather than gold currency became an accepted 'standard of exchange' used in trading – merchants, traders knew a 'Promissory Note' always had enough gold value behind it to prove its worth; this note could be exchanged for gold at any time.

A 'Promissory Note,' is just one method, which has progressed to the widely used card system of the 21st Century.

The plastic card systems are taking over the coin and note currency market in the 21st Century.

Cards can work as either Promissory Notes, (credit cards) or Debit Card.

Debit Card

The Debit Card system is supposed to represent the old coinage system – you can only spend what is left on the Debit Card!

Credit Cards – Debt To The User

However, the Credit card is different and works on an amount of perceived credit you have held in the bank's system. Every time you use the bank's credit system, if the credit isn't cleared monthly, you are charged a fee, often with escalating interest!

Regardless of the system used, people still want to know they are receiving value for the money they spend.

The Gold Standard

I have said earlier in this book, 'When you are selling, you need to sell the story'. Money too, has its own and unique story.

When the coinage system was first developed by the Lydian King, Croesus in 635 BC and thereafter, used for many centuries, gold was seen as the accepted way of buying goods or services. The gold currency system later revealed it too, was flawed and open to abuse.

For many centuries, and because of the crude system of manufacturing coins, the coins could be interfered with. This interference came about through people cutting small but significant edges from the minted gold coins.

In the Seventeenth Century, this process was known as 'clipping'. The 'Clippers' as they were called, depleted the true value of the coin.

Again, because the gold value of the coins had been reduced, the merchants and consumers were in turmoil not knowing the true value of the goods or services they were buying or selling.

A remedy to the situation was found in the seventeenth century by Sir Isaac Newton who developed the Gold Standard.

The Gold Standard system invented by Newton included the coins being made by a machine invented in France and installed in the Tower Of London. Prior to this time, all coins were hand-made. The newly minted coins had a thicker, named or numbered edge. This reduced the 'clipping' of coins, they therefore retained their value.

Borrowings Against The Gold Standard

The Gold Standard secured borrowing. The Gold Standard is a monetary system in which the standard economic unit of account is a fixed weight of gold.

In the United Kingdom, the Gold Standard was steadfast until the beginning of the First World War in 1914.

'The Gold Standard allows for checks and balances to occur and limits government spending which limits the amount of debt that can accumulate within a country'.

Free Market

This is a broad and diverse area of economics and I am not an economist! As you know, I specialise in writing 'How To' books on human behaviour. My books are intended to be used as tools for self-development in business or personal development. However, I need to introduce an end to this book on Selling.

Though I grew up in a 'Free Market' economy, my sensitivity to how money works and human behaviour has come about through my own life experiences in business and education.

I believe the interest of these two remarkable areas developed when I was very young. I remember the rationing of goods in the fifties; rationing included: eggs, bread, milk and meat.

Even at a very young age, the experiences have left their mark on the way I think and work.

Rationing finalised in England in 1954 - meat was the final item to be taken off the rationing list.

My research reveals a 'Free Market' is a market where the government does not interfere or intervene or regulate supply, demand, and prices.

A 'Free Market' is left to regulate itself through the mechanism of buying and selling goods, stocks or commodities in the market place – a 'Free Market' is controlled by the markets in which it operates.

'Free Market' economies need to operate with honesty, integrity and transparency, if they do not exhibit these qualities, the 'market place' goes into 'free fall' and spirals downwards to destruction as it did in 2008.

Thank you for buying this book and taking your time to read it.

Writing on such a diverse subject allows me to keep expanding my own learning – every book I write has its own unique story behind it.

The story, the hours of research and the pulling together of thoughts and ideas all create and add to the quality of my own life and wellbeing and strangely enough, lead me to the next book to be written.

Thank you again for your time.

Christine Thompson-Wells

YOUR NOTES

Bibliography

A. J. Andrea Ph.D., *World History Encyclopedia, Volume 2*, ABC-CLIO, 2011, ISBN 1851099301,

Bernstein, P The Power Of Gold – DVD A Tinopolis Production for S4C International in Association with France 5 and RTE © 2003.

Haralambos, et al Psychology In Focus, Causeway Press, PO Box 13, Ormskirk, Lancashire, L39 5HP 2002

Richmond, V.P., & McCroskey, J.C. (1998). Communication: Apprehension, avoidance, and effectiveness, 5th ed.. Boston, MA: Allyn & Bacon.

Schaller, K. (2002). Principles of effective public speaking: Student workbook. Boston, MA: McGraw-Hill.

For more information, please go to:

www.booksforreadingonline.com

www.ingramcontent.com/pod-product-compliance
Lightning Source LLC
Chambersburg PA
CBHW051539010526
44107CB00064B/2780